How To Get A Teenager To Run Away From Home

BY MARTIN A. RAGAWAY

illustrated by Don Robb

a ~~Laughter Library~~ book

PRICE/STERN/SLOAN
Publishers, Inc., Los Angeles
1983

SIXTH PRINTING — AUGUST 1983

Copyright © 1980 by The Laughter Library
Published by Price/Stern/Sloan Publishers, Inc.
410 North La Cienega Boulevard, Los Angeles, California 90048

ISBN: 0-8431-0537-2

Put a picture of
yourselves on his wall.

Leave little scraps of
soap in her bathroom so
when she washes her
face, she'll swallow it.

*Get a mother-daughter
outfit and follow her
around wherever she goes.*

Remodel the kitchen.

On Halloween, suggest that she go trick or treating — as is.

Give him a gift certificate for a vasectomy.

Leave him with only wire
hangers in his closet and
reverse every other one.

*Find out what his/her
special hobby is. . . and
get interested in it.*

Stick labels on cartons
of milk: ''NOT TO BE
TAKEN INTERNALLY.''

Put the cat's litter box in
his room.

Play the Bee Gees album
at 16 rpm.

Get the maternity
hospital where he was
born to tell him he's
being recalled because
he has a screw loose
somewhere.

Constantly remind him
that when you were his
age you worked 12
hours a day. (Also
pretend not to hear him
when he says, "I'm
glad you finally
developed the wisdom
to stop it.")

Lead him to believe that
you've made a
reservation in Stockholm
for a sex change operation.

Deduct withholding tax from her allowance.

If there's a large mean dog next
door, line his pockets with chopped liver.

Tell him you've made
appointments for
conferences with all
his teachers.

Replace his bed with
bunk hammocks.

Walk around the house naked...

*Paint a target on his
favorite t-shirt.*

*Put a purple organdy canopy
over his bed.*

*Hang around when his
friends come over. Tell
him you want to be one
of the boys.*

Reset all the push buttons on his car radio so that it only gets news and classical music.

Get her to clean up her room by temporarily "misplacing" her tickets to the rock concert.

Make her 20 minutes early for everything by setting her clock 20 minutes ahead. That should get her ticked off.

Tie knots in her dental floss.

Start borrowing her panty hose.

*Offer to pay her if she'll
give you whining lessons.*

Put a vending machine in his room. . . but keep no change around the house.

Put a TV camera on the ceiling and have it scan the room every 30 seconds.

Keep asking him if he'd like to be traded to another family for a draft choice to be named later.

Figure out what it would cost to send him to college and offer it to him in cash. . . if he leaves immediately.

While he's asleep, put a Teddy
Bear's head at the foot of his bed.

Get a guard dog and
don't tell him that he
goes for the throat
when he hears the
words, "Is he
friendly?"

Insist on helping with
homework.

Put up a "No Smoking"
sign. . . and fill his water
bed with liquid nitrogen
gas.

*Start every
conversation with. . .
"When I was your age. . ."*

Hang a picture of a
stork in the living
room, with the caption,
*"WHAT CAN I SAY
DEAR, AFTER I SAY
I'M SORRY."*

*Make her go to the
prom with her 12-year-
old cousin.*

Go on the make for her
boyfriend. . .

Write to the Department of Agriculture and find out if the government will pay you *not* to raise him.

Insist on giving him a haircut at home.

*Hide the auto polish so
he can't simonize his teeth.*

Put a sign on his car, **"NOTICE TO THE FUZZ.
YOU CAN KISS MY REAR."**

At the dinner table remind him constantly, ". . . when I was your age do you know how many hours I had to work to make a dollar?"

Hold a garage sale in his bedroom.

Paste pimples in the center of his mirror.

Hire a plumber to get his
toilet to flush up.

Put a sign on the bedroom door which reads,

PART–TIME HUMAN BEING.

Tell him he just received a scholarship from the University of Lima in downtown Peru.

Have the telephone cord so that while it's possible to sit on the bed and use it, you can't lie down and talk.

Starch his jockey shorts.

Straighten up *her* room so she can't find anything.

Let him know that you've made an appointment with the doctor to have him wormed.

Show her friends baby pictures of
her lying on a bearskin rug.

*Don't hesitate to let
them know your true
feelings. Say things
like, "The trouble with
you is that one minute
you're here. . . and the
next minute you're
here."*

Get friendly with his
girlfriend's parents.

Whenever you think of it, tell her she'll always be "Daddy's little girl."

Hang a dead albatross from his shower rod.

Draw a moustache on his Farrah Fawcett poster.

Burn her John Travolta picture.

Tell her that she's not adopted; that you're her real parents.

Wash her tennis shorts and then dry them on a poison sumac bush.

Put a sign in the bedroom:

A TEENAGER IS AN ADOLESCENT WHO ACTS LIKE A BABY WHEN YOU DON'T TREAT HIM LIKE AN ADULT.

Never enter his room without wearing a gas mask.

In the middle of the night — while he's asleep — sneak into his room and pour a cup of water in his bed.

Take the door off his room.

Leave a tube of Preparation H in the toothpaste glass.

Take all the mirrors out of the room. . . so it's impossible to practice smiling.

Fold up the hide-a-bed and yell "Earthquake" while he/she is still in it.

Suggest they have a disco party. . . and come down in your day-glo slacks.

Take a power drill and enlarge the hole in her favorite records by 1/16 of an inch.

Put a lock on the **outside** of his bedroom door.

Fill his hair spray bottle with Nair so his long hair will fall out.

Hand him the keys to a neighbor's Corvette. . . tell him to try it and see if he likes it. Then notify the police that it's been stolen.

Leave a travel brochure from Holland in his room and on it write, "Pot is legal in Amsterdam."

Turn the refrigerator around. . . with the door to the wall.

Fix the gas gauge in his car so it always reads "full." This way he may run out of gas, God knows where.

Hire a beautiful well-built Swedish maid and tell him she's gay.

Spill grape juice on his favorite disco shirt.

Let him think you've made a deal with the CIA to have him assassinated.

On Halloween, don't buy a pumpkin. Make him stand outside the house.

Stock the refrigerator
with beer and put a lock
on the bathroom door.

Stretch Saran Wrap over the toilet in his john.

Put Vaseline on the outside door knob so when he comes home he can't get into the house.

Smear gravy on his face while he's asleep so that the dog will lick his face all night.

Iron his jeans and put a crease in them.

Put a note in his room:
"The laboratory called.
The rabbit didn't die, but
it's still in intensive
care."

When she's away for the
weekend at a girlfriend's
house, send her this
telegram: DON'T
RETURN HOME. ALL
WILL BE FORGIVEN.

*Adjust her scale so it
registers 5 pounds
more every day.*

Make yourself available for advice before you're asked.

Fix him up with dates. . . with the children of *your* friends.

Invite her teacher to dinner.

At the next family
gathering, make him kiss
all his aunts and uncles.

Serve bean sprouts on
their Cheerios.

Sign their report cards with an X.
(Because you don't want the teacher to think he comes from a home where the parents can read and write.)

Let him know that you're going to the PTA meeting wearing a disguise.

Knit holes in his socks.

Fill his sneakers with
sweet cream, so while
walking to school he can
churn butter.

Set fire to the welcome
mat and throw it in the room.

*Put a school of piranha
in his waterbed.*

Hide the Clearasil until she cleans up her room.

When she comes home dust her for fingerprints.

Under a large picture of
him, put the sign,
POSTER BOY FOR
POPULATION ZERO.

Serve boiled codfish for
dinner, 40 nights in a row.